OUR SOLAR SYSTEM
JUPITER
THE BIGGEST PLANET

by Mari Schuh

pogo

Ideas for Parents and Teachers

Pogo Books let children practice reading informational text while introducing them to nonfiction features such as headings, labels, sidebars, maps, and diagrams, as well as a table of contents, glossary, and index.

Carefully leveled text with a strong photo match offers early fluent readers the support they need to succeed.

Before Reading

- "Walk" through the book and point out the various nonfiction features. Ask the student what purpose each feature serves.
- Look at the glossary together. Read and discuss the words.

Read the Book

- Have the child read the book independently.
- Invite him or her to list questions that arise from reading.

After Reading

- Discuss the child's questions. Talk about how he or she might find answers to those questions.
- Prompt the child to think more. Ask: Jupiter is covered with stripes, spots, and swirls. What are these shapes on Jupiter? What causes them to move and change?

Pogo Books are published by Jump!
5357 Penn Avenue South
Minneapolis, MN 55419
www.jumplibrary.com

Library of Congress Cataloging-in-Publication Data

Names: Schuh, Mari C., 1975- author.
Title: Jupiter : the biggest planet / by Mari Schuh.
Description: Minneapolis, MN: Jump!, Inc., [2023]
Series: Our solar system | Includes index.
Audience: Ages 7-10
Identifiers: LCCN 2022027125 (print)
LCCN 2022027126 (ebook)
ISBN 9798885243490 (hardcover)
ISBN 9798885243506 (paperback)
ISBN 9798885243513 (ebook)
Subjects: LCSH: Jupiter (Planet)—Juvenile literature.
Classification: LCC QB661 .S37 2023 (print)
LCC QB661 (ebook)
DDC 523.45–dc23/eng20220913
LC record available at https://lccn.loc.gov/2022027125
LC ebook record available at https://lccn.loc.gov/2022027126

Editor: Jenna Gleisner
Designer: Emma Bersie

Photo Credits: AliveGK/Shutterstock, cover (background); Elena11/Shutterstock, cover (Jupiter), 23 (left); muratart/Shutterstock, 1; Nerthuz/Shutterstock, 3; Pictorial Press Ltd/Alamy, 4; Kevin M. Gill/NASA/JPL-Caltech/SwRI/MSSS, 5; Tristan3D/Shutterstock, 6-7; joshimerbin/Shutterstock, 8-9, 12-13, 14-15 (Jupiter), 19; Thomas Thomopoulos/NASA/JPL-Caltech/SwRI/MSSS, 10; Evgeniyqw/Shutterstock, 11; Sergio Lucci/Shutterstock, 14-15 (background); Nemes Laszlo/Shutterstock, 16-17; NASA/JPL-Caltech, 18; NASA, ESA, CSA, Jupiter ERS Team, 20-21; HAKAN AKIRMAK VISUALS/Shutterstock, 23 (right).

Printed in the United States of America at Corporate Graphics in North Mankato, Minnesota.

For Paige

TABLE OF CONTENTS

CHAPTER 1

A HUGE PLANET

One night in 1610, **astronomer** Galileo Galilei used a **telescope** to look at Jupiter. He noticed something others had not. He saw four moons **orbiting** the **planet**.

telescope

Galileo Galilei

Jupiter is the biggest planet in our **solar system**. How big is it? All other planets in the solar system could fit inside it!

Jupiter is much bigger than Earth. If Earth were the size of a grape, Jupiter would be the size of a basketball.

Earth ····▶

Jupiter is the fifth planet from the Sun. Take a look!

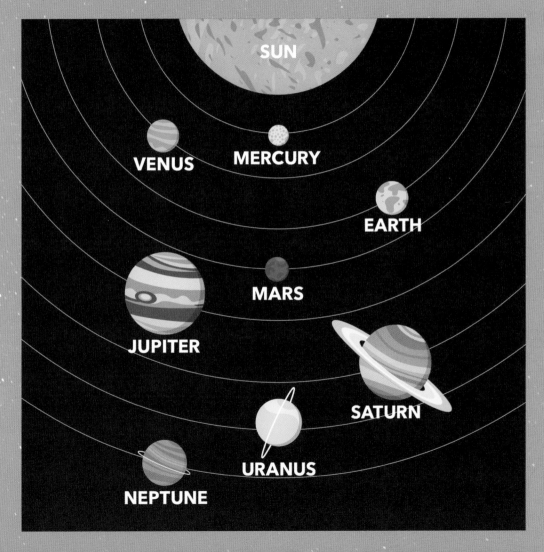

All planets spin. One full spin is one day. Jupiter spins faster than any other planet in our solar system. This means it has the shortest days. One spin, or day, on Jupiter is less than 10 hours!

DID YOU KNOW?

Jupiter has the highest **gravity** of all planets in our solar system. Why? A planet's gravity depends on its size, **mass**, and **density**. Jupiter has the most mass.

CHAPTER 2

ALL ABOUT JUPITER

Jupiter is covered with stripes, spots, and swirls. These shapes are clouds. They float in different layers of Jupiter's thick **atmosphere**.

Jupiter is a stormy, windy planet. Its winds are stronger than any on Earth. Strong winds push the clouds around.

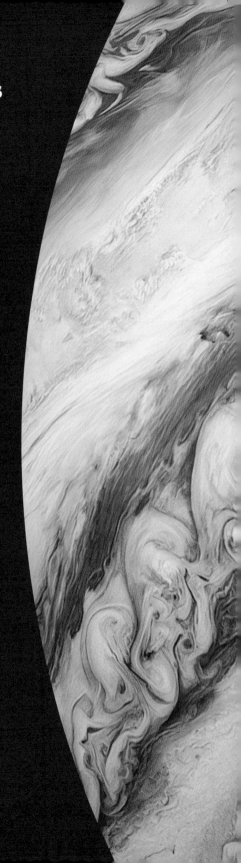

A huge storm is on Jupiter. It is bigger than Earth. It is called the Great Red Spot. It has lasted hundreds of years.

DID YOU KNOW?

Jupiter has the biggest ocean in the solar system. It is deep in Jupiter's atmosphere. It is made of hydrogen.

Great Red Spot

Jupiter is one of the gas giants. It is made up almost entirely of gases. It does not have a solid surface. Hot, thick liquid is deep inside the planet. Scientists think Jupiter's **core** may be solid. The core might be very hot. It could be 43,000 degrees Fahrenheit (24,000 degrees Celsius)!

TAKE A LOOK!

What is Jupiter made of? Take a look!

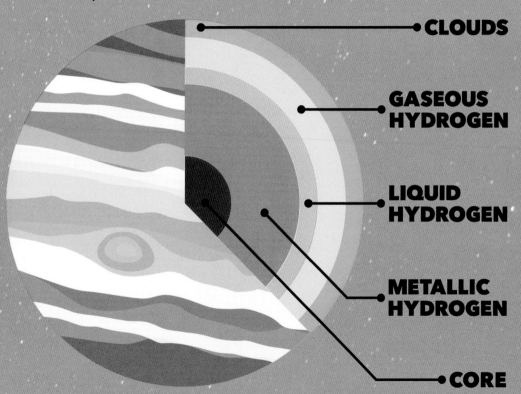

CLOUDS

GASEOUS HYDROGEN

LIQUID HYDROGEN

METALLIC HYDROGEN

CORE

Ganymede

Jupiter has at least 79 moons. Its biggest moon is Ganymede. In fact, Ganymede is the biggest moon in the solar system! It is bigger than Mercury.

CHAPTER 3

AMAZING DISCOVERIES

In 1979, *Voyager 1* and *Voyager 2* were **launched** into space. They both studied Jupiter. They discovered that the planet has rings made of tiny rocks and dust. The thin rings are hard to see.

Voyager 2 launch

The **spacecraft** discovered three new moons. They also discovered **volcanoes** on Io. Io is one of Jupiter's moons.

Io

rings

In 2022, the *James Webb Space Telescope* took new images of Jupiter. The images are very clear. They show Jupiter's rings!

There is more to learn about Jupiter. What more would you like to discover about this planet?

DID YOU KNOW?

In 1995, the *Galileo* spacecraft became the first spacecraft to orbit Jupiter. It put a **probe** near the planet. The probe gathered data about Jupiter's gases.

TRY THIS!

STORM IN A BOTTLE

Huge storms and strong winds are found on Jupiter. Make your own storm in this fun activity!

What You Need:
- clear bottle with a cap or a jar with a lid
- water
- liquid dish soap
- food coloring or glitter (optional)

1. Fill the bottle or jar more than half full with cold water.
2. Add a few drops of liquid dish soap.
3. Add food coloring or glitter if you wish.
4. Tightly twist the cap on the bottle or jar.
5. Shake the bottle or jar quickly, using a circular motion. What happens? What do you see inside?

GLOSSARY

astronomer: A scientist who studies stars, planets, and space.

atmosphere: The mixture of gases that surrounds a planet.

core: The center, most inner part of a planet.

density: The measure of how heavy or light an object is for its size. Density is measured by dividing an object's mass by its volume.

gravity: The force that pulls things toward the center of a planet and keeps them from floating away.

launched: Sent into space.

mass: The amount of physical matter an object has.

orbiting: Traveling in a circular path around something.

planet: A large body that orbits, or travels in circles around, the Sun.

probe: A tool or device used to explore or examine something.

solar system: The Sun, together with its orbiting bodies, such as the planets, their moons, and asteroids, comets, and meteors.

spacecraft: Vehicles that travel in space.

telescope: A device that uses lenses or mirrors in a long tube to make faraway objects appear bigger and closer.

volcanoes: Mountains with openings through which molten lava, ash, and hot gases can erupt.

Ganymede

Io

INDEX

TO LEARN MORE

Finding more information is as easy as 1, 2, 3.

1 Go to www.factsurfer.com

2 Enter "Jupiter" into the search box.

3 Choose your book to see a list of websites.

FACT SURFER